# *Poetically* SPEAKING

Tierra J. Hummons

*Everything I write is from what I have experienced.*

*I believe in being authentic.*

*My best work comes from my testimony.*

# CONTENTS

# CONTENTS CONT.

# CONTENTS CONT.

## *ACKNOWLEDGMENTS*

I am very thankful to have the opportunity to self-publish

my second book. I give God all the honor and praise for

my accomplishments. He is the reason for my success.

Also, I want to thank my very close family and friends for

their continuous love and support. It warms my heart to

see my dreams come true.

## *Real Love*

You never have to fight for real love.

Love comes naturally.

If you ever find yourself fighting for it to stay,

Then it is not real.

What is meant for you will be for you.

You will never have to force it to stay.

You do not have to find real love.

Real love will find you.

Love is genuine.

Love is happiness.

Love is comforting.

Love is peace.

Love is everlasting.

True love is real.

## *Pride*

I wish you would let go of your pride.

Call me up and let's go for a ride –

To hash out our differences and get back on good terms.

I never want us to end.

I just want you to learn –

Learn from your mistakes.

Forever be real with me.

Treat me like a queen.

Love me endlessly.

I just want you to let go of your pride.

You keep hiding your feelings –

But I know you have a heart deep down inside.

## *Too Much*

We live in a world where too much becomes too little

And too little becomes too much.

Everyone is afraid to compromise

So, they would rather give up.


Men are afraid to give in –

Women give in too much.


There's a constant battle between egos

And women are left to feel

Like they are not enough.


All she ever wanted was to be loved unconditionally

By a man she could trust.

He wasn't ready to be with one person.

She was asking for too much.


All she ever wanted was to grow

With her significant other.


He wanted to grow alone –

So, she was asking for too much.


She never asked for fancy dates,

Diamond rings, big houses, or monetary gifts.

She just wanted an everlasting companion

Who she could build with.


Too much became too little.


Too little became too much.

A selfish man will never obtain the skills

To satisfy her love.

## *Beautiful, Black Queens*

This message is for my beautiful, Black queens

Who have determination and ambition.

This is for my Black queens who are goal-driven

And values their self-worth.


If a man isn't taking the necessary steps to keep you happy,

Make you feel special, and solidify your position in his life,

Then you do not need him.


You are a beautiful, Black queen with substance.

That is very rare in this society.


If a man wants to drop the ball

And miss out on something great —

A once in a lifetime opportunity,

Then it is his loss.


Never be afraid to cut ties with an individual

Who is going to hinder your growth or steal your joy.


You deserve peace.


You deserve happiness.


Most importantly, you deserve a man

Who is going to love you consistently –

Without any limitations.


So, never jeopardize your heart

For a temporary situation.

People come and go,

But your happiness should last forever!

## *A Prayer for Him*

Last night I prayed for you.

I asked God to meticulously craft a man

Who was meant for me.

I want nothing, but the best.


Last night I prayed for you.

I asked God to wrap His protective arms around you.

I want you to always be safe.


Last night I prayed for you.

I asked God to build your strength and solidify your peace.

Your physical and mental health matters.


Last night I prayed for you.

I asked for your relationship with the Heavenly Father

To continuously grow.


I prayed for your success, happiness, and maturity.


I prayed for us.


Last night I prayed for you,

Because someday we will become one flesh

When we walk down the Holy aisle and say,


"I do."

## Don't

Don't tell someone to be happy,

When you are depressed.

Don't tell someone to know their worth,

When you are always settling.

Don't tell someone to forgive others,

When you are still holding onto the past.

Don't tell someone to be honest,

When you are constantly lying.

Don't tell someone to be slow to anger,

When you are not quick to kindness.


Moral of the story is:

You cannot make someone else whole,

When you are half empty.

### ...he can

He loved you at the beginning with all his heart.

He made you feel special.


Then he gives you 90% of effort

While you still give your full one hundred.


You keep quiet and you do not ask for more,

Because you know he will never fall short again.


Time goes on – he only gives you 35%.

You still give 100%.


Eventually you decide to throw in the towel,

But he comes back for another chance.

You welcome him with open arms,

But he disappoints you again.


You think he still loves you – each time he comes back.

Yet, he only comes back – because he knows he can.


He knows you will not require any extra effort,

Because you are so comfortable with his presence.

He knows you would rather settle

Instead of moving on.


He loves you with little effort,

Because he can.


He will never change and leave you disappointed,

Because he can.

He treats you however he wants,

Because he can.


If you continue to stay –

You will never get what you deserve.

## The Wrong Time

We met at the wrong time.


We were young, and ready to fall in love.

I was ready for forever,

But he had doubts or whatever.


I just couldn't understand

How I could meet the right person

At the wrong time.


See – whether it's the right time or the wrong time –

What I feel in my mind –

Is that we were meant to be together.

We could make it through the stormy weather.

We weren't picture perfect,

But we were perfect for each other.

I would never replace him with another,

Because he was mine.

However, it was the wrong time.

He was on a different path

And I was on another.

I'm still trying to figure out how to recover –

From the bad timing.

I'm trying to figure out

How I can turn the wrong time into the right time —

And take the right steps to make him all mine.

Yet, I had to check out of fantasy

And check into reality.


God obviously had other plans for me.

I must follow God's directions.

I must wait for God to bless me.


Whether we were meant to be together or not —

He will always remain special to me,


But unfortunately —

It's the wrong time.

## *Two Different Paths*

He wasn't secure enough

To handle a magnificent woman like you.

He had to water down your angelic character

To feel comfortable in your presence.


You were everything he could need or want,

But he wasn't capable of understanding that.


He admired you from afar,

Then as he got closer your brilliance scared him.

He didn't believe he deserved someone special,

Because he lacked confidence.


You were on a path to greatness.

He struggled to match your progress.

Instead of admiring you from afar,

He chose to be selfish

By guiding you in a deceptive direction.


Although he wasn't secure enough

To value a woman like you,

He couldn't bear to watch someone else have you.


He was on a different path,

But he would do anything to get you to follow him.

## *Effortless Society*

What happened to the society

Where people admired nature rather than technology?

What happened to the society

Where children carried toys and coloring books,

Instead of iPhones and tablets?


Technology has diminished our creativity,

Communication skills, and intelligence.


We no longer bring meaningful conversation

To the dinner tables,

Because we would rather bring our phones instead.


Teenagers no longer care to call

And check on their grandparents,

But can spend hours playing games

Or seeking popularity from social media.


What happened to the mothers who raised their daughters

To become women with ambition and self-respect?

What happened to the fathers who raised their sons

To become men with intelligence and dignity?


We no longer have a society filled with successful doctors,

Authors, dancers, painters, scientists, chefs, lawyers,

Mathematicians, engineers, or anything of substance.


We have lost our values and individualism.

We no longer own any morals.


There are more females in our society

Who want the benefits of a family,

But do not demand to have a ring.

There are more males in our society

Who want the benefits of a relationship,

But refuse to own a title.


We have lost the value of marriage, everlasting relationships

And meaningful friendships.

We lack generosity, unconditional love, and family support.


Did we ever have a society of substance?

Did a meaningful society ever exist?


We live in a society that lacks the efforts

Of striving for greatness.

Unfortunately, an effortless society is the new norm.

We hate to compose an expressive essay

For a literature class,

But we can easily write a longwinded post on social media

To entertain a crowd who will never benefit us.


What have we become?

Were we ever in a state of excellence?


An effortless society is what we live in

And hope is what we have lost.

## *One Life*

You only get one life.

Not two or three,

But only one.


Your life will become great

When you stop living for everyone else

And start living for yourself.


Dare to be different.

Think more and fear less.


Stand out in the crowd.

Go after everything you deserve.

Step outside of your comfort zone

And live your life like there is no tomorrow.


Tomorrow may come,

But you may not be alive to see it.


So, start living for today.

Tomorrow can worry about itself.

## *Special Gifts*

Everyone has a talent.

These talents are special gifts given to us by God.

It may take certain people longer than others

To figure out what their talent is,

But we certainly have them.

God gave us these gifts to please Him

And to inspire our peers in unique ways.

When we use our gifts to bless others –

God will use His power to bless us.

## *Midnight Thoughts*

I want the best in life.

I want everything I deserve,

But I must experience growth

To receive the blessings God prepared for me.


I want to be successful.

I certainly want to make my family proud.

I want to give back to the people who gave to me.


I want to smile more and cry less.

I want a life with less stress and more paychecks.


I have so many goals to accomplish

And so many dreams to fulfill.

I could never settle for less.

It's midnight –

And my mind is racing with different thoughts.

I see success in my future,

But I must stay focused

And keep my eyes on the prize.

## *The College Advice*

College is the start of a new journey in your life.

It can be an exciting time, if you allow it.


This new journey is a time to explore who you are,

Become more responsible, meet great people

And enjoy new opportunities.


College is extremely different than high school

On many levels.


High school is mandatory,

While college is optional (for most people).

However, the biggest difference between the two

Is the time frame to complete your education.

Never let your pride tell you

It is mandatory to graduate "on time."


You may want to graduate with your original class,

But that is not guaranteed.

People change their majors, transfer to different colleges,

Take a semester off, and unexpected circumstances

Will happen.


College is not a race – it is simply a marathon.

You can finish at your own pace without the need to rush.


Earning a degree is a major achievement

That most individuals cannot accomplish.

So, it does not matter how fast you finish.

Completing college and earning a degree

Is the most important goal!

If you do not finish in a short time frame, you will not fail.

You only fail when you completely give up.


So, do not stress, make wise decisions

About the courses you take, and do not

Overload your schedule.


Most importantly, finish college at your own pace!

## Diverse Nation

We can learn from each other,

When we let go of fear and practice humility.


We cannot change the past,

But we can certainly learn from it.

Nothing happens overnight,

But progress begins with a single action.


One problem Americans have

Is their quickness to assume.


When we make assumptions,

The American society loses the opportunity

Of embracing different cultural and ethnic groups.

This causes us to remain divided,

When we are supposed to be united.


We must be willing to learn about people

Who differ from us

And this starts with asking questions.


Some individuals are opposed to asking questions,

But questions are very important.


When we ask questions,

We receive answers.

When we receive answers,

We can gain an understanding of something

We once knew nothing about.


Yes, we must ask questions.

However, we must be aware

Of how we ask those questions.


In most cases, it is not what we say that can be offensive –

But how we say it.


It is impossible to be culturally competent

Due to constant societal changes.

Yet – it is extremely important

To have cultural humility and awareness,

When living in a diverse nation.


We may come from different backgrounds,

But we all live in the same country.


So, embrace diversity!

It will forever exist.

### *...we wouldn't make it*

They said we wouldn't make it.

They said we would always be in chains —

But my God.

We are free.


They said we would always call them "master,"

But the true master is God.


They said we wouldn't amount to anything,

But we had the courage to fight for our freedom.


They said we would never be intelligent,

But WE built this country,

We gave speeches.

We wrote books.

We designed new structures.

We led a revolution.

We became innovative

And we paved the way to our future success.


They said we would never receive a proper education,

But we have more degrees and PhDs

Than they could have ever imagined.


We went through the violence.

We suffered from oppression.

They tried to silence us,

But our voices grew louder.


They tried to take everything from us.

They gave us nothing –

But we STILL managed to turn that into something.


We still face many barriers today —

But that will NOT stop us!


We are here.

We are strong.


They said we wouldn't make it.

They said we would always be in chains —

But my God.


We are FREE!

### *Father*

A father will not harm his children

Physically or mentally,

But he will love them unconditionally.


A father knows his children

Needs guidance in every direction.


They need more than love and affection.

They need a strong man who is always present.


A father will not let his children down,

Because failure is useless.


His children need support and less excuses.

A father will make a way for his children

Just like the mother.


He must solidify his position

Before he is replaced by another.


A father will never harm his children

Physically or mentally.


He will always love them —

Unconditionally.

## *"Black Lives Matter!"*

It's okay for us to vandalize our own neighborhoods,

But when the White man does it —

"Black Lives Matter!"


It's okay for us to steal from our brothers,

But when the White man does it —

"Black Lives Matter!"


It's okay for us to disrespect our mothers,

But when the White man does it —

"Black Lives Matter!"


It's okay for us to kill our own,

But when the White man does it —

"Black Lives Matter!"


When we kill our own, we show the world

That it's easy for them to kill us too.


Life is precious

So, when it's taken

That pain is hard to get through.


We say we want justice.

We say we want peace,

But we are the reason for the violence

In our OWN streets!


Black Lives do matter,

But we must SHOW it.

The world will never take us seriously,

If we don't own it.


How can we expect them to love us,

When we don't love ourselves?

How can we expect them to believe our words,

When we don't believe in us?


It's okay for us to destroy each other,

But when the White man does it —

"Black Lives Matter!"

## All Cried Out

They say when it rains –

It pours.


This is certainly true.


If anyone is feeling pain,

I understand –

Because I'm feeling it too.


I've cried so many tears

I can build my own lake.


If anyone ever said life would be easy,

I'm here to set the record straight.

Life will never be easy.

I'm still going through –

I wish my happiness was more

And my pain was few.

I feel another storm getting closer.

I no longer have any fear.

I've cried so many times

I think I'm running out of tears.

God please hear me –

I'm all cried out.

I'm lost.

I'm confused.

I need You to tell me what these storms are about.

I'm tired of the struggle.

I don't know if I can make it each day.

I need You to open Your heart

And listen while I pray.

God I truly need You.

I don't want to have any doubts.

I can't face another storm.

I'm all cried out.

## *When I Cared...*

When I cared,

It stressed me out.

When I cared,

I started overthinking.

When I cared,

Nobody else did.

When I cared,

I experienced more pain.

When I cared,

I was disappointed.

So, now I no longer care.

I'm not a heartless individual,

But I no longer worry about the unchangeable.

I have no more energy left to give.

## *Empty*

I gave a piece of me to everyone who entered my life.

I gave my happiness.

I gave my love.

I gave my loyalty.

I gave my compassion.

I gave my time.

I gave my effort.

Unfortunately, I gave my heart to people

Who didn't deserve it.

I was so consumed with keeping everyone else happy,

I forgot to put myself first.


I gave too much, and I received too less.

It left me feeling empty.


I had nothing left to give.

I had nothing left for myself.


I prayed and asked God to refill me

With His unconditional love.


I asked God to fill the void within my heart.


I asked God to help me become strong enough

To leave the door closed on individuals

Who don't deserve a welcome into my life.

Feeling empty is never fulfilling.


I deserve to feel complete

And I will never jeopardize my wholeness again.


Never fully give yourself away to anyone, except God.

Always save a piece of you for you.

## *Different*

He looked me in my eyes

And told me he was different.


I didn't believe him,

But a part of me thought he meant it.


I promised myself I wouldn't show him any attention,

But he wouldn't let me go.

He remained persistent.


He begged for my valuable time and commitment.


I even opened my heart so, he could see what was in it –

But as soon as I gave him a chance

He took my love to waste it.

The signs were clear when he became complacent.

Now I'm back where I started
I'm hurt once again –

By another person who pretended to be my friend.

I hope he enjoyed this game,
Because this will be the last time he wins.

I should've never let my guard down.
I should've never let him in.

He looked me in my eyes
And told me he was different –

But it was only a selfish plot to get my attention.

## *Everything*

I gave him everything,

But he still found another woman more attractive.

He still found another woman more entertaining.

He still found another reason to devalue my love.

I was everything he ever wanted.

I was everything he ever needed in a woman,

But that still wasn't enough.

I simply could not satisfy a confused man.

Although he couldn't find the courage to love me,

I still knew he was one compared to MILLIONS.

I may not have been everything to him,

But I know I will be everything and MORE

To the right man.

## *It's Not You, It's Him*

He lied.

He cheated.

He broke you down inside.


He destroyed your peace

And took you on a painful ride.


It's not you, it's him.


He told the lies.

Never let that heartless man kill your pride.


He pinned the blame on you

To erase the guilt from his mind.

He was selfish.

He was careless.

He did not value your time.

It's not you, it's him.

He chose to ruin the best thing he had.

It's time to put yourself first

And leave him in the past.

# *Defeated*

I was lower than low.

I was at the bottom of the bottom.

I reached the darkest moment of my life and I felt defeated.

I kept pushing.

I kept fighting.

I kept reaching for any source of light

Shining in my direction –

But the darkness was too overpowering.

I climbed up just to get knocked down.

I tried climbing again, but I was left feeling defeated.

I cried.

I screamed.

I grew angry at my failures.

I was determined to reach the top,

But I had no idea of how to get there.

I tried every option possible –

Only to fail repeatedly.

I was low.

I was lost.

I was defeated.

## Redefining Self

I must stop letting my flesh get the best of me.

God said He'll take care of me.


I must be patient and keep my faith,

Because blessings come unexpectedly.


God never promised life would be easy,

But He promised to remain present.


I must fix my life on earth so,

I can gain my wings and make it to heaven.


It's not enough to be a good person.

I must surrender my all

And give my life to Christ.


Jesus died to save my soul

And to erase my sinful plight.


I just want to redefine my life.


I'm just trying to make everything right.


When judgement day comes –

I just pray the Heavenly Father knows my name

And I'm not excluded from the Book of Life.

## Who Am I to Complain?

I have not been through it all,

But I have certainly been through a lot.

Yet – I am still standing.


I have been in some situations

That no one else could handle.

I even endured pain with a smile,

Because I knew I was still blessed despite my struggles.


So – I am a strong, young woman.


Life is not perfect,

But it is always better than what it could be.

I used to think I had a tough life

Whenever I faced a bad storm,

But God always reminded me that I was beyond blessed.


I only faced a few storms,

While others were facing daily storms.

This is not to say my storms were less difficult.

However, I had more to be thankful for.


Yes, I went through some frightening battles,

But I didn't have it as bad as the woman

Who was raped by the person she trusted.


I didn't have it as bad as the man

Who was physically and mentally abused

His entire childhood

And never received the love he deserved.

I didn't have it as bad as the Syrian boy

Who watched his family get brutally murdered.


I didn't have it as bad as the mother

Who had to depend on a homeless shelter

To keep her children safe.


I didn't have it as bad as the old Haitian man

Who never knew what his next meal would be.


I certainly didn't have it as bad as the little girl

Who was given up to multiple men for sex

By her drug-addicted mother.


So, who am I to complain?


I had some weary days,

But I would rather walk a thousand miles in my own shoes

Without any breaks

Before I chose to walk in someone else's.


We have all been through a struggle and experienced pain.

These trials were not meant to break us,

But to build our character and inspire others.


Whenever you catch yourself feeling down,

Think about your blessings and ask yourself –


"Who am I to complain?"

### Redemptive Mind

I felt defeated as I sat in darkness.

Although I tried every alternative to reach the light,

I instantly failed.

I had redemption on my mind,

But I was losing hope.

Suddenly, I heard a voice from God telling me to try again.

However, I was too afraid of being a failure.

Then God told me I was not a failure,

Because I never gave up.

You only become a failure when you stop trying,

But I never stopped trying.


However, I did everything my way

Instead of God's way.


God presented routes to the light,

But I thought my path was better and easier.


Unfortunately, I was wrong.


An easier path would not allow me

To become stronger and wiser.


I had to submit to God.


I had to trust Him

To guide me through the darkness.

Redemption was on my mind

And through God I would never fail.

## *Surrender*

God is perfection.

There is nothing perfect outside of Him.

God will never forsake us.

He will never hurt us.

He will never place more on us than we can bear.

Yes, God will allow us to go through

Trials and tribulations.

It is beneficial for our growth.

God only wants to love us, protect us

And save us through the name of Jesus.

So, why would we ever want to run

From an unconditional love?

God gives us more chances than we deserve –

To change our lives and surrender to Him.

When we choose not to listen,

God will quickly change our atmosphere

To get our attention.

He will take everything away from us

Where our only choice is to submit to Him.

If we still choose to disobey God

During this crucial moment,

We are setting ourselves up for failure.


We become our own worst enemies,

When we choose to stray away from God.


When we do not surrender our all,

We must be prepared to fall.

## Never Lose Faith
### *(Inspired by Romans 5:1-5)*

How can we call ourselves believers when we have lost hope in the Heavenly Father, who loves us unconditionally despite our numerous flaws?

God kept us when we didn't keep ourselves. God loved us when we didn't love ourselves. God blessed us when we never deserved it.

God gave us strength when we didn't have the courage to continue living. God protects us every day, and grants us new mercies by the grace of His Holy Son.

So, why have we lost hope?

Why do we no longer keep our faith? God never promised we would have an easy life, but He promised He would never leave us during our toughest storms.

Everyone goes through a time when they feel defeated and hopeless. I too, have experienced this dark moment. It was mentally, spiritually, and sometimes physically painful.

I was overwhelmed, and I felt alone even when I was surrounded by a room full of people. I was losing my happiness. I was losing my motivation. I was starting to forget who I was.

However, God encouraged me to look to Him. Without God's mercy, I would not be where I am today. I would not have the strength, faith, knowledge, and wisdom I finally have.

I would be empty and incomplete without God.

Although tribulations are burdensome, they are necessary for our lives. Without our tribulations we would not be able to grow into the wonderful human beings God planned for us to be.

We would become complacent, and we would never be great. Without our tribulations we wouldn't be able to persevere.

If we can't persevere, we can't produce character. If we can't produce character, we don't have hope. Without hope our faith is lost.

So, if the Bible tells us that God will give us peace because of hope, then why do we worry?

How can we worry when we serve a God who can turn nothing into something?

God's children will always be protected and taken care of.

He granted us that through His Holy word. If we can depend on God, we can depend on His word. If we can depend on His word, we do not need to worry.

I went through a time when I worried myself to sickness and depression. There was a time when I wanted to give up on my dreams.

I was in a very dark place, but it was only God who lifted me out of that sorrow. He pushed me to my Bible, and gave me strength to read. When I gained my strength, I was able to keep going.

God's perfect work can only be done when we decrease ourselves and increase Him. When we're going through our tribulations, it is hard to look over the bridge and see victory.

Yet, we will continue to hope for the best when we have faith. If the sun shined every day, we would become ungrateful. If the rain poured every night, we would become hopeless.

There is a need for balance to appreciate the blessings we receive in our lives.

God never makes any mistakes.

He knows when to bless us, and He knows how much we can bare.

So, don't be surprised by trials and tribulations. Not only is this a chance for us to pass another test, but it's also a chance for us to fully trust in God.

It's during our darkest moments when God can work a miracle by turning the impossible into possible.

This is when God can show us who He truly is, and why He deserves all the honor and praise!

Without our unfortunate circumstances, we would not be able to grow into the individuals God has planned for us to be.

We would not reach our maximum potential, if we never knew how it feels to fall.

Also, we would not possess the Godly wisdom needed to survive on this earth, if we never had a chance at redemption.

We must keep our faith as we are walking through the darkness to get to the light.

If we keep the faith, God will become our eyes and see us through any pain we may endure. If we keep the faith, God will become our strength when we grow weary. If we keep the faith, God will provide the sunshine after the rain.

I am a living testimony of how God lifted me from the darkness and brought me to victory.

I would not be able to speak or write on this subject, if I did not experience this for myself.

I used to crack under pressure. I used to fall when pain would cross my path, but now I am no longer afraid to face a storm.

If I got through it once, I can get through it twice.

I can get through any storm when I have Jesus by my side!

I thank God I am not where I used to be, and I am not who I used to be. I have grown so much, and my growth is due to my tribulations.

My tribulations helped me persevere. When I persevered, I developed character. When I developed character, I produced hope.

Never doubt God, because He can perform miracles no human being could ever think of.

Never let your darkness consume you.

Never stop seeking salvation from the Lord.

Most importantly, NEVER lose faith!

*Our experiences give us our greatest wisdom.*

*Do not let them defeat you, but allow them to inspire you.*

## *ABOUT THE AUTHOR*

Tierra J. Hummons was born on January 13, 1996 in Dayton, OH. She has written poems since the 5th grade. Tierra's interest in poetry inspired her to self-publish her first book, *The Poetic Soul* in May 2017.

She is also interested in motivational speaking and health-related studies. However, her true passion is for liturgical (praise) dancing to glorify God.

Tierra graduated from Stivers School for the Arts in 2014, then she attended Eastern Kentucky University. After 2 years of attendance at EKU, she transferred to a different institution.

Tierra currently attends The Ohio State University as a Public Health major. Once her undergraduate studies are complete, Tierra plans to attend graduate school at OSU for Nursing.

With her Public Health and Nursing degree, Tierra plans to start a career at Nationwide Children's Hospital.

Her goal is to become a nurse practitioner – specializing in pediatrics and a public health educator to continue helping the lives of others.

Made in the USA
Monee, IL
13 July 2020